Unsp... History

The Untold Story of the Jackson/Curling Family and Their Lives as Canadian Home Children

Historian's Note

During the late summer of 2014 Diane Kirby contacted me as part of her efforts to update the Reynold's Plantation Ladies Club Resource and Services Book. I was listed as a trusted tradesman. An historian. While verifying my information, we engaged in a conversation regarding what I actually do, and she was intrigued by the possibility that I might be able to create a document chronicling the story of her family.

And an interesting story it is! As you will soon find for yourself as you read on. What she told me was amazing. Her ancestors had come from England to reside in Canada. Like many other immigrants one might think. But with her story there is a sad twist. Through hardship and tragedy at home, Diane's grandmother and two of her siblings would be taken from the arms of their mother in England and shipped off to Canada to work as indentured servants. All in the name of what Victorian England considered "charity."

Diane provided me with a lot of documents and several excellent books related to the thousands of English children who were similarly uprooted and resettled, and specifically relating to her own relatives. These documents were copies of the handwritten ledger books kept by the supervising institution regarding each child in their custody and care.

It is wonderful to be provided with such source documents. There are, however, some shortcomings found in any such documents. First, they are handwritten and it was not always easy to read the variety of handwriting styles found therein. Second, some of the people making entries in the ledgers provided better, more detailed information than others. Third, on a couple of occasions I found entries that were contradictory or confusing, and at other times I found that there were gaps in the information caused by missing entries, missing documents or just plain old bad recordkeeping.

Given this, I have put together the following story which primarily chronicles the lives of the three children sent to Canada, but also includes information about those who stayed behind, relatives who went before them, and those who came after them. I have also included some information on the "Home Children" adventure as a whole and the world as it existed in England and Canada during the late 19th and early 20th centuries. As much of the information is from ledger books, I have endeavored to make each entry sound as if it were written by Dr. Barnardo himself, without losing the meaning of the words.

I want to thank Diane for her interest in this subject, and for entrusting the creation of this document to me.

Matt Alexander

Curiosity

Most of us have an interest in where we came from and who our ancestors were. This knowledge gives us a sense of knowing ourselves, and better understanding our relatives. It also can offer a sense of pride in our family. Perhaps our ancestors did great things. Or maybe they overcame great obstacles just to survive. Whatever the case, they are our family.

In 2004 Diane Kirby began the process of finding her ancestors through Barnardos. To find any information she had to submit a request, filing a form with her name and address, who she was inquiring about, if she were the nearest surviving relative of that person, and as much information as she had about the name, date of birth, location of birth, time of entry into the home, where they sailed to and departed from, their parent's names and any specific questions she wanted answered by Barnardos. In other words, she had to have already done some homework!

Diane promises in her letter that she will not be emotional or upset about any information that she receives, she just wants the information on her family history. She already had an inkling that there might be something buried in the records that could be unpleasant.

Her grandmother and her sister and brother said very little to their families about their youth and Barnardos experiences. "Family secrets" that were not talked about. Now Diane and the family would like to fill the gaps and understand what their relatives went through. Perhaps this might explain some of their actions as adults.

Barnardos was very helpful and they sent nice long letters explaining the results of their inquiry, detailing what is enclosed and why. They sent copies of original documents, written over many years in several hands, to get a better idea of the family background. There were also photographs of each subject person included.

They were also very strict in saying that this is all very confidential information and it needs to be kept private. Therefore, it is not to be shared. They went so far as to say that if the information were shared with family members, they would prefer that the Barnardo name not appear on the documents.

The people at Barnardos also say that the wording in the documents can sometimes sound quite judgmental and that the facts may cause discomfort, that is "pain and distress on first reading".

Initially, Diane was only able to obtain the records of Florence Gertrude Jackson, her grandmother. This was because it was known that Diane was in fact the closest living relative. In the case of her Grandmother's sister, Alice Maud Jackson, Barnardos could not release any information because it was not known exactly who the nearest living relative was.

In January of 2005 Barnardos determined that Diane Kirby was Alice's nearest surviving relative and therefore provided her information to Diane.

In The Beginning

Out of the mists of time, and through the famous fog of London, the picture of the Jackson family begins to emerge late in the nineteenth century. It is at this point that we find solid records of the people and places that formed the family. Working class tradesmen, building the modern foundations of England in the Industrial revolution. Every life story, in the very beginning, is filled with the prospect of hope and prosperity, as was the life of this family. But the journey of life takes many twists and turns, and in the case of this family, tragedy, illness and separation lead to a story that would seem to be impossible to us today. A story that turns out to be not uncommon for people of that time and place, but very much hidden from public view.

In this story we will follow the path from John Robert Curling and his wife Elizabeth down to the present day. While there will be information regarding as many of the branches of the tree as possible, that is, those for which there is documented information, the primary path to be followed will be that coming from John and Elizabeth down through their daughter Florence Gertrude Jackson.

It is her story that is of particular interest in that she represents the life of tens of thousands of children whose fate was largely hidden from the world. A life defined by England's need for Empire Building, and the greed and lack of human compassion that came with it. Hers was a life formed by her experience as human chattel. A white slave. One of the tens of thousands of children who experienced Barnardos and its brand of charity for the poor and homeless.

The Foundations

In the late 1800's, England was a Matriarchy, ruled by Victoria, Queen of England and Empress of India. That being the case, the family history will begin on the maternal side with Ellen.

The year 1863 saw the Battle of Gettysburg in the raging Civil War of the United States, but in England it was highlighted by the birth of a baby girl to loving parents John Robert Curling and his wife Elizabeth Donahue Curling. Named Eleanor, the child would come to be known more familiarly as Ellen.

Eleanor Curling (Ellen) Jackson was born in Rotherhithe in 1860 or maybe 1863 per second source. (See discrepancy below). The name "Rotherhithe" derives from the Anglo-Saxon *Hrȳðer-hȳð* meaning "landing-place for cattle." The first recorded use of this name was in about 1105, as *Rederheia*. In the past Rotherhithe was also known as *Redriff* or *Redriffe*, and is a residential district in southeast London, England, and part of the London Borough of Southwark. It is located on a peninsula on the south bank of the river Thames, facing Wapping and the Isle of Dogs on the north bank, and is a part of the Docklands area. It borders Bermondsey to the west and Deptford to the southeast.

Rotherhithe has a long history as a port, with

many shipyards from Elizabethan times until the early 20th century and with working docks until the 1970s. In the 1980s the area along the river was redeveloped as upmarket housing, through a mix of warehouse conversions and new-build developments. The rest of Rotherhithe is now a rapidly gentrifying residential and commuter area. Because much of the former Surrey Docks had strong trade links to Scandinavia and the Baltic region, the area is still home to a thriving Scandinavian community.

Others of note with ties to this area of London include actor Michael Caine who was born Maurice Joseph Micklewhite in Rotherhithe. Eliza Fay (1755 or 1756-1816), author of *Original Letters from India* (1817), was born in Rotherhithe. Thomas Coram (1668-1751), a philanthropic sea captain, retired to Rotherhithe where he campaigned for the establishment of the Foundling Hospital. Aaron Manby assembled and launched the world's first seagoing iron-hulled ship at Rotherhithe in 1822. Alfred Hitchcock filmed scenes for his first film as director, *Number 13* (1922), in Rotherhithe before it was pulled from production.

This area has notable ties to significant and pop culture events. In July 1620, the *Mayflower* sailed from Rotherhithe for Southampton on the south coast of England, to begin loading food and supplies for the voyage to New England. In the popular television drama series *Upstairs,*

Downstairs the character James Bellamy stands as a Conservative Party candidate for the constituency of Rotherhithe East. Redriff was the fictional birthplace of Jonathan Swift's character Lemuel Gulliver, of *Gulliver's Travels* fame, and where his family waited for him. Rotherhithe is alluded to in the British Sea Power song *Carrion* and the Elvis Costello song *New Amsterdam*. The final chapter of Charles Dickens's *Oliver Twist* (1839) provides a lively depiction of a Rotherhithe slum-district of the mid-19th century. In "The Adventure of The Dying Detective", Sherlock Holmes pretends to Dr. Watson that he has contracted a contagious disease in Rotherhithe, while working on a case.

On Valentine's Day of 1869 Ellen Curling was christened in St. Nicholas Church in the Deptford area of London. St Nicholas' Church, the original parish church, dates back to the 14th century but the current building is 17th century. The entrance to the churchyard features a set of skull-and-bones on top of the posts. A plaque on the north wall commemorates playwright Christopher Marlowe, who was murdered in a nearby house, and buried in an unmarked grave in the churchyard on 1 June 1593.

Ellen Curling married Albert Jackson during the first quarter of 1888 at Greenwich in greater London, Kent, Surry. At first they lived at 93 Childeric in Greenwich, Deptford. This was a residential area of row houses about a mile from the river Thames and less than two miles from the Royal Observatory of Greenwich, the home of the zero latitude line.

Albert Jackson was a bricklayer. Little is known of his life other than that he was married to Eleanor "Ellen" Curling, that they had five children together, he worked for Ellen's father, who was a builder in a small way, that he was addicted to drink and that because of him the family was thrown into turmoil.

Ellen Curling Jackson and Albert had five children together. From oldest to youngest they were Ellen Edith "Nellie" (1888), Alice Maud (1889), Albert William Jackson (1891), Florence Gertrude (1893), and Frances Rose (1894).

After ten years of marriage tragedy struck the family when on April 19, 1898, Albert Jackson committed suicide by hanging himself at their home at 35 Darfield Rd, Brockley. This is currently a residential district of row houses. Of interest is that not far from this area, at the time of Albert's death, would have been the palatial homes of the captains of industry of the time.

As a thirty-five year old widow with five young children, Ellen Curling Jackson found times to be very hard indeed. She was forced to move to 1 Merritt Road, Brockley, where all six of them lived in one room. Ironically, this location is on the next road over from Darfield Road, the place where Albert died. On July 12, 1898, she made a very painful decision and sent three of her children off to Barnardos, to further move on to Canada.

Barely hanging on for three months, Ellen Curling Jackson was offered a very painful solution to her circumstances. In July of 1898, one of the only social service available at the time stepped in. The church. They conducted an inquiry into the family circumstances and found that "Ellen, a charwoman, is of excellent character but poor health having had two surgeries for internal abscesses.   Since her husband's death she has earned 6 shillings per week by charring, and pays 4 shillings for the rent of one room. She is still suffering from a tumor," and it was felt that the maintenance of the two remaining children was as much as she was equal to, even with the help received from the Parrish and from her father.

Barnardos, a charitable organization that took in orphaned and homeless children, was contacted shortly thereafter. Rev W. H. Mason, 6 Montague Avenue, Beckley, brought the case of the children to their attention. He agreed to get a grant from the Parrish of 5 shillings per week if Ellen's father would match that amount. Her father agreed, but is already heavily burdened. Three times married he has eighteen children! Five of whom still live at home, one a helpless invalid needing special help. To support all of this, the man's earnings are 40 shillings per week.

The church made the decision that the children should be removed from Ellen's home and sent to Barnardos. It was decided that Ellen Curling Jackson could keep her oldest and youngest children, while the three middle children would go to Barnardos. It was felt that at age ten, the oldest was old enough to care for the youngest, aged 4, and the two of them could remain with their mother in England.

Florence Gertrude Jackson, aged five, was separated from her mother and two siblings, and sent off with her sister Alice Maud and brother Albert William to a new and frightening world. Albert left for Canada as of March 21, 1901 and Florence and Alice left September 19, 1901.

On September 20, 1901 Ellen Curling Jackson receives a letter stating that her two daughters have sailed to Canada. On October 14, 1901 she gets another letter saying they have all arrived safely.

The 1901 census from London, taken in April of that year, shows that there was an Ellen Curling Jackson, aged 44 (should have been 41) living in Greenwich. Ellen Edith "Nellie", the oldest, and Frances Rose, the youngest, would still be with her at this time.

Ellen Curling Jackson went to Canada with Nellie and Rose probably in 1907 to find the other three children. A 1910 Toronto city directory put her living and working in a restaurant at 103 Church Street. The 1912 Toronto city directory has her at 267 Church Street. She might have had a grocery store at DuPont and Chrisie before 1928. After this Ellen Curling Jackson moved to California with Nellie (the oldest child) to meet up with Rose (the youngest child) who had emigrated to the United States in 1921.

Ellen Curling Jackson died in June of 1926 in Venice, California.

The World in 19th Century England

During the 19th century, London was transformed into the world's largest city and capital of the British Empire. Its population expanded from 1 million in 1800 to 6.7 million a century later (1.9% average annual growth). During this period, London became a global political, financial, and trading capital. In this position, it was largely unrivaled until the latter part of the century, when Paris and New York City began to threaten its dominance.

While the city grew wealthy as Britain's holdings expanded, 19th century London was also a city of poverty, where millions lived in overcrowded and unsanitary slums. Life for the poor was immortalized by Charles Dickens in such novels as Oliver Twist.

History

The practice of sending poor or orphaned children to English and later British settler colonies, to help alleviate the shortage of labor, began in 1618 with the rounding-up and transportation of one hundred English vagrant children to the Virginia Colony in the Americas. In the 18th century, labor shortages in the overseas colonies also encouraged the kidnapping of children for work in the Americas, and large numbers of children were forced to migrate, most of them from Scotland. This practice continued until it was exposed in 1757, following a civil action against Aberdeen merchants and magistrates for their involvement in the trade.

The Children's Friend Society was founded in London in 1830 as "The Society for the Suppression of Juvenile Vagrancy Through the Reformation and Emigration of Children". Simplified, this suggests that the children were rounded up and shipped off in order to rid the streets of London, Liverpool and Belfast of the increasing number of street urchins known as street Arabs. In 1832 the first group of children was sent to the Cape Colony in South Africa and the Swan River Colony in Australia, and in August 1833, 230 children were shipped to Toronto and New Brunswick, Canada.

The main pioneers of child migration in the nineteenth century were the Scottish Evangelical Christian, Annie MacPherson, her sister Louisa Birt, and Londoner, Maria Rye. While working with poor children in London in the late 1860s MacPherson was appalled by the child slavery of the matchbox industry and resolved to devote her life to these children. **Home Children** was the child migration scheme founded by Annie MacPherson in 1869. Under this program more than 100,000 children were sent from the United

Kingdom to Australia, Canada, New Zealand, and South Africa through several agencies including Barnardo's.

In 1870 McPherson bought a large workshop and turned it into the "Home of Industry", where poor children could work and be fed and educated. She later became convinced that the real solution for these children lay in emigration to a country of opportunity and started an emigration fund. In the first year of the fund's operation, 500 children, trained in the London homes, were shipped to Canada. McPherson opened distribution homes in Canada in the towns of Belleville and Galt in Ontario and persuaded her sister, Louisa, to open a third home in the village of Knowlton, seventy miles from Montreal. This was the beginning of a massive operation that sought to find homes and careers for 14,000 of Britain's needy children.

Maria Rye also worked among the poor in London and had arrived in Ontario with 68 children (50 of whom were from Liverpool) some months earlier than McPherson, with the blessing of the Archbishop of Canterbury and *The Times* newspaper. Rye, who had been placing women emigrants in Canada since 1867, opened her home at Niagara-on-the-Lake in 1869, and by the turn of the century had settled some 5,000 children, mostly girls, in Ontario.

Enter Thomas John Barnardo, born in 1845 in Dublin, Ireland. Barnardo went to Catholic school where he was beaten and this influenced his attitude toward children. From an early age he was seen as a determined person and this determination would take him far, but also bring him many enemies. In 1863 Barnardo becomes an evangelical Christian and member of the sect of Plymouth Brethren. With utmost determination Barnardo sets out to find a way to save souls.

He began by preaching and got interested in becoming a missionary to children in China. To train for this he took up the study of medicine at London Hospital. He worked hard but was not really devoted to this work. He soon lost the favor of those people doing recruiting for China missions and quit medical school. But he continued to call himself a doctor.

He became an evangelist to children at first focused on their souls and not their well-being. In 1870 he decided that the boys on the street needed more than food and clothes, they needed a real home so that their steps could be set upon the path of righteousness. He bought a house in Stepney, refurbished it and had room for 70 boys. He went out in the streets and found boys and by September 17, 1870 he had 25 clean scrubbed boys. On that day he led them in a simple service and that was the beginning of his home.

At first his position was to take in only as many boys as he could afford, but he was deeply touched by the death of a boy he had turned away and changed his motto to "no destitute child ever refused admission." His home provided for the boys in a Spartan way but they had food and clothes and shelter and schooling. And they learned a trade, partly to raise money to fund Barnardo's operation, but also to prepare them for life on the outside. He also used them for a messenger service in London. They were known as the City Messenger Brigade. Each boy wore a uniform of tunic, striped pants and a hat looking like that of a Salvation Army officer.

The emigration schemes were not without their critics and there were many rumors of ill treatment of the children by their employers and of profiteering by the organizers of the schemes, particularly Maria Rye. In 1874 The London Board of Governors decided to send a representative, Andrew Doyle, to Canada to visit the homes and the children to see how they were faring. Doyle was a renowned lawyer with a background in the conditions in which the poor lived. In June of 1874 he went to Canada to check on the children.

Doyle's report was published in February of 1875. In it he praised the women and their staff, especially MacPherson, saying that they were inspired by the highest motives, but condemned almost everything else about the enterprise.

He said that the attitude of the women in grouping together children from the workhouses, who he said were mostly of good reputation, with street children known as street Arabs, who he considered mostly thieves, was naïve. This practice had caused nothing but trouble in Canada and had given the entire Home Children program a bad name.

He was also critical of the methods by which children were placed with families and of the checks made on the children after they were placed with settlers. Canadians would apply for a child, with little done in the way of a background check being done, and would receive a child at random, with no thought given to the many factors which would influence the success or failure of the placement. As far as post placement checks, which in Rye's case were mostly non-existent, he said that:

Because of Miss Rye's carelessness and Miss MacPherson's limited resources, thousands of British children, already in painful circumstances, were cast adrift to be overworked or mistreated by the settlers of early Canada who were generally honest but often hard taskmasters.

He also took issue with the post placement supervision of the children. Maria Rye had no follow-up with her children or the family they were placed with. And many of these children just vanished. McPherson would send a friend out to visit the family and check on the child, but this was much more as a social visit to the family than anything else.

The one bright spot he saw on the operations was that children under the age of 5, who were too young to be worked, were adopted and were mostly adopted by sincere people who treated them well. These children did well.

The Canadian House of Commons subsequently set up a select committee to examine Doyle's findings and there was much controversy generated by his report in Britain, but the schemes continued with some minimal changes and were copied in other countries of the British Empire. On the other hand, Canadians were incensed by his report and rallied round Rye and McPherson. Politicians knew they needed these children for cheap labor to grow the country and defended the women. They said the women had good intentions, were Christians and didn't need any more follow up or better systems. In effect, they were of the mind that England could just butt out.

They went so far in their efforts to discredit Doyle that he became the focus of their attack. They called him a deadbeat and a leech. A Catholic even who was interfering in Protestant business. They thought the children were of a lesser class than themselves. These were not children at all, but just workers. These English children were guttersnipes and coming to Canada was the best thing that ever happened to them.

This was certainly odd talk coming from people who had the same Anglo-Saxon blood coursing through their veins.

Meanwhile, back in England, Dr. Barnardo had arrived and was recognized in London as a man of deep religious zeal and moral commitment, and as a brilliant administrator and fundraiser.

In the summer of 1873 he got married and was then ready to begin work with homeless girls. He built a group of fourteen cottages that he called the Girls Village Home because he believed the girls would do better in smaller groups.

His success brought jealousy from competitors and they began attacking him for calling himself a doctor, for bad money management, for alleged cruelty to children and, most shockingly, for living with a prostitute before he was married.

In 1881 he took a dozen or so of his boys to Anne McPherson and she took them to Canada. In 1882, after weathering the storm of the above attacks, he sent his first group over to Canada under his own program. Dr. Barnardo had learned a great deal from Anne McPherson and now was on his own.

Barnardo goes to Canada to see his operation in 1884. He hopes to help remove the negative feelings about the children and to see that he was indeed sending his kids off to a better life. He insisted that his children were different from those coming in under other programs. They were carefully trained, carefully selected and carefully placed and supervised.

He travelled across Canada and visited many of his children, especially the girls. He would ask the host farmer if his ward was a good girl and then ask her if she was being well treated by her master and mistress.

In the year 1887 Barnardo's empire is expanding and he opens Barnardo's Industrial Farm in Manitoba, western Canada. His idea was that boys 17 years of age and older would go out to the farm and work, would then get hired by other farmers, and eventually would start a farm of their own. Barnardo's Farm was to be profitable, and indeed was, but mainly the graduates went to work for other farmers rather than starting their own farms.

BARNARDO GIRLS' CANADIAN OUTFIT
— 1898 —

new box
label
key
stationary
brush and comb
haberdashery
handkerchief
Bible
hymn book
2 stuffed dresses (blk/gold)
2 print dresses
2 flanelette n' dresses
2 cotton n' dresses
garters
shoe and boot laces
tooth brush
brush and comb
8 small towels in bag

2 pr. hoses (thick)
2 pr. hoses (thin)
2 flanelette petticoats
1 winter petticoat
1 summer petticoat
2 coarse aprons
2 holland aprons
2 muskin aprons

ulster
tom o'shanter
hat
1 pr. boots
1 pr. oxfords
1 pr. slippers
1 pr. plimsolles
1 pr. gloves

Courtesy — F. Rightmeyer

BARNARDO BOYS' CANADIAN OUTFIT
— 1930 —

1 peaked cap
1 suit
1 pr. rubber soled boots
1 pr. slippers
2 long nightshirts
2 pr. woollen socks
1 pr. overalls
1 set light underwear
2 shirts

2 pocket handkerchiefs
1 pr. braces and one belt
1 ball of wool for sock repairs, needles and thread, boot brush
1 Bible
1 marked New Testament
1 Travellers Guide
1 Pilgrims Progress

Courtesy — W. A. Eyden

A list of items provided to each child before they departed for Canada.

J. J. Kelso hit the scene in 1887 with the opinion that children are human and need protection. Surprisingly, the Canadian government takes his side, forms the Children's Aid Society and in 1893 passes the first bill in Canada to protect children.

Kelso realized that the influential people of Canada, as well as the courts, churches, and the police had confidence in the groups doing child placements, but also knew that they had some concerns about the homes being careless with the children, trusting too much in human nature in believing that the people of Canada were all good and would treat the children well, and not checking on them after they were placed.

By 1895 attitudes in Canada were changing toward the children coming to Canada from England. At the beginning everyone thought it was a wonderful idea even though there was a general perception that Britain was dumping her worst children in Canada. The children were thought to be generally inferior. But now, some economic downturns had caused rising unemployment among the adult men of Canada and these children were seen as taking jobs from these men at reduced, even free, labor cost. It was organized labor saying this, but politicians and newspapers jumped on this bandwagon and painted a picture of all of these children as criminals or freaks. The Canadian government used their own data to paint a different picture, but the caricature was there and instilled hard.

The labor groups also challenged the philanthropists as profiteers and for a while the children were banned from school (even though that was part of their contract) and in the extreme the children were generalized as the carriers of syphilis and painted as violent criminals and thus were greatly feared.

Dr. Barnardo returned to Canada in 1887, 1890 and 1900 to observe the work of his staff and assess the success of his efforts. He always went to meet with his children. And the children always seemed glad to see him, flocking to him when he visited. Dr. Barnardo always seemed to remember each of them. Most graduates had fond memories of him and his homes, just not of Canada after they were placed.

Barnardo died 1905. His empire began to fall apart in 1908 when the industrial farm was split up and sold off. His vision lives on though, and today Barnardo's is still serving as the United Kingdom's largest children's charity. They no longer run orphanages, but instead work with children and their families in the community, giving them the practical and emotional support they need to deal with disadvantage.

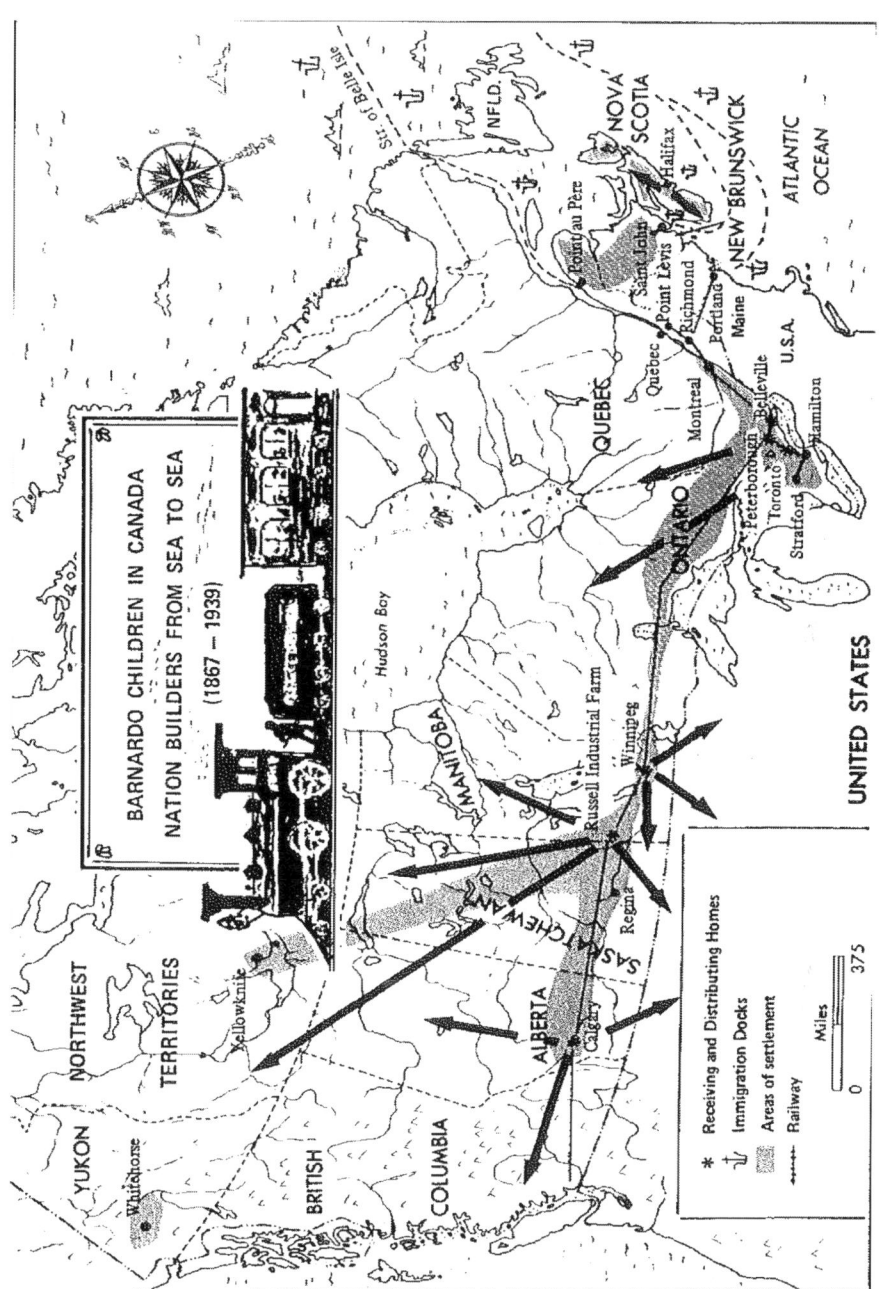

This map gives an indication of the distribution of Barnardo's children throughout Canada.

The SS Tunisian, the ship that brought many of Barnardo's children to Canada from England, including Florence Gertrude, Alice and Albert Jackson.

Frederick Curling

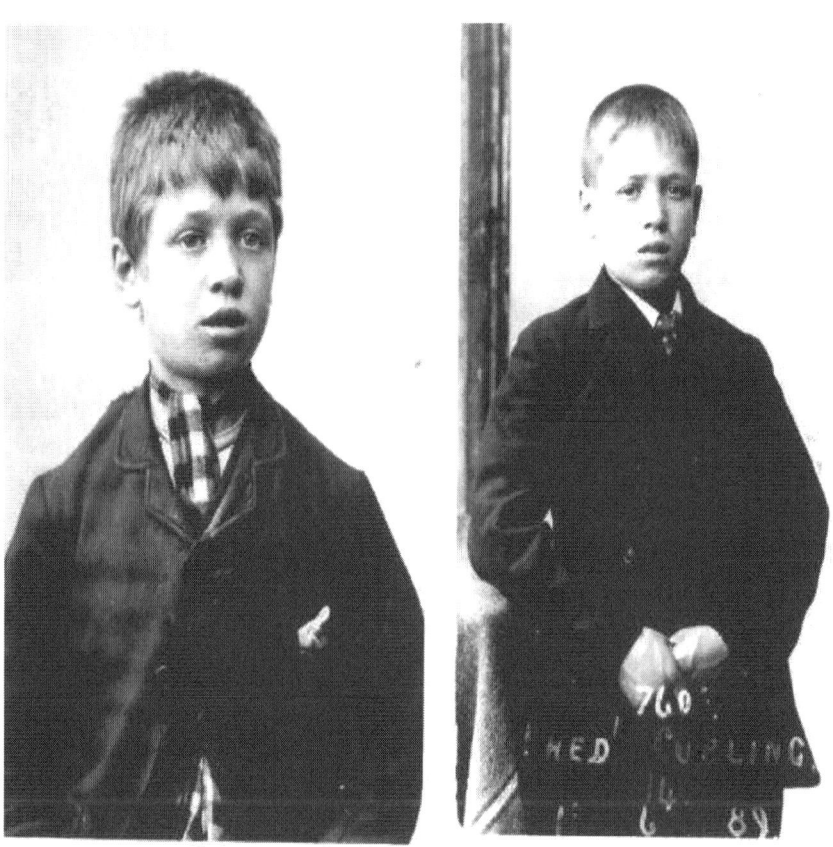

Frederick Curling on his admission to Barnardo's, October 13, 1888, and again, clean and shiny, heading off to Canada on June 13, 1889

Frederick Curling was the first member of the extended family to make the trip to Canada via the Barnardo's system. In the family tree,

Frederick was an uncle to the Jackson children, the son of Ellen Curling Jackson's sister Elizabeth. As an uncle, he was a number of years older than the Jackson children.

Born June 5, 1875 in Deptford, South London, Frederick was the second son of Elizabeth Curling and John Curling. James was the name of his older brother and he was three years senior to Frederick. There were also four daughters in the family.

At age thirteen, Frederick and his family found themselves in dire straits. His mother was employed as a needlewoman earning three shillings per week (the equivalent of one quarter of a pound which even at todays exchange rate is about forty cents in U S dollars) and living with the two boys in a single room at 1 Finch Street, High Street, Deptford. To earn additional income she occasionally worked as a nurse. Her ability to work at all was limited as she was partially paralyzed and could hardly scrub or wash. In spite of this she was recognized in the community as a respectable woman.

She had separated from her husband several years prior as their marriage was not one made in heaven. He was addicted to drink, and she had a bad temper. John Curling, aged 61, was also known as Johnny Kanarr. At this time he is working as a dock laborer living in a common lodging house at 127 Grove Street in Deptford.

His income is very unstable, much as he is himself. He is aged looking, weak and almost past work. He suffers from rheumatism and a broken leg. He does contribute a trifle on the rare occasions when he is able. There is no hope of reconciliation between Elizabeth and John.

The three shillings Elizabeth earns per week is hardly enough to cover the rent let alone provide for her and two boys. As stated, there were four daughters. Amelia James, aged 30, was married to a journeyman tailor. They had six children and lived at 80 Bell Street, Henley-on-Thames. Elizabeth Biswell, aged 21, was married to a laborer. They had two children and lived at 17 Taunton Road, Burnt Ash Lane, Lee. The youngest daughter was Frances Curling, aged 16. She worked as a general servant to a family living at 161 Lynton Road, Dockhead. And then there was Ellen Curling Jackson. At age 23 she found herself in a marriage with a bricklayer. They had one child at that time and lived at 16 North Road, New Cross. When they were able, daughters Ellen Curling Jackson and Elizabeth would assist their mother with money and food.

Finding herself in these circumstances, Elizabeth petitioned Barnardos to take the two boys. To offer them a better life. James had turned 16 and had recently found a situation as an errand boy to the baker on High Street, Mr. Vohman. He earns 6 shillings per week. With this turn of events, Elizabeth believes that she and James can make it as a family, but only without Frederick.

Fred is healthy, intelligent and of good disposition. He has gone to school passing the sixth standard at Hughes Fields Board School. On his intake papers he was described as 13 years, 4 months of age with fair hair, blue eyes, and a ruddy complexion. He stood four foot and five and three quarter inches tall and was thin, weighing 73 pounds. His right front lower tooth is broken and decayed. And now he finds himself leaving his family and making his way through the Barnardo's system.

Frederick was admitted to Barnardos on October 3, 1888. He spent one night at the receiving house in Stepney and was then transferred to Kinnaird House, which was also in Stepney. On June 13, 1889, Frederick sailed with a group of other children in similar circumstances to Canada on board the SS Vancouver. They arrived in Quebec on June 23, 1889 to begin their new lives.

Very shortly after his arrival, Frederick is placed on June 25 with a Mr. John Dickinson, Esquire. Mr. Dickinson lives in Barrie, near Toronto.

Staff members working for Barnardo in Canada provide the following history of their experience with Frederic through a series of journal entries.

June 25, 1889 (Fred is 14 years old) Mr. Dickinson writes complaining that Fred is badly affected with ringworm and has also a sore hip. The boy says the sore on his hip is cancer. Dickinson indicates that Curling is a nice, well-mannered little fellow and regrets that he will have to return him to us.

June 25 We received a telegram later in the day from Mr. Dickinson stating that he will keep the boy.

July 3 Mr. Dickinson writes that Curling promises to turn out a good boy being quiet, hardworking, and biddable. Dickinson is very pleased with the boy.

July 3 Mr. Dickinson writes to say that he has taken Curling to a physician who states that the sore on Fred's hip, which the boy said was cancer, is actually caused by a poverty of blood. Good news. (This may have been a reference to what is known as scurvy. A metabolic disorder caused by the lack of vitamin C which can be found in areas afflicted by extreme poverty. Very treatable when diagnosed.)

August 30 Mr. Dickinson writes to request that he cannot keep Curling in his employ any longer. He states that the boy is of a very low type character and will only attend to his work when under somebody's immediate view. He is also a persistent liar, and so dirty in his habits that the other servants object to taking their meals with him. Mr. Dickinson will return the boy to us on 2 September.

September 1   Mr. Dickinson writes to say that he will give this boy another trial. He is thinking that perhaps with further patience and care, he might improve.

September 21   Fred has returned to us. Mr. Dickinson writes that Curling, who is incorrigibly idle and deceitful, has no ambition to learn or try to work and is as irreclaimable as a wild animal! Added to this, Mr. Dickinson says the boy has been dishonest. Mr. Dickinson greatly regrets that his efforts to do something for the boy have proved futile.

September 30   Frederick is still in our Toronto home.

October 1   Our Frederick Curling has been sent to Mr. James Storey of Pakenham, Ontario.

October 21   The Reverend Partridge of Pakenham informs our man, Mr. Owen, that Mr. Storey is well satisfied with Curling who is doing well. Mr. Storey will keep the boy for four years at a wage of 30, 40, 50 and 80 dollars per year. The boy is quite willing to remain under these conditions.

November 2   Mr. Storey informs us that Curling objects to the financial arrangements we have made with all of our children in that he does not like any balance of his wages being sent to us at the home. Curling is content to remain where he is if he may receive his wages directly.

November 29   Mr. Storey writes that he cannot sign Curling's contract since the boy has an objection to his wages being sent to us at the home.

December 25   Christmas Day. Frederick Curling writes to us that he is in good health, and that he has gained 20 pounds in weight since going to this place.

February 26, 1890 (Fred is 14 and a half years old)   Mr. Storey writes to us that Curling does not suit him and asks for the removal of the boy at an early date.

August 16   Our Mr. Owens has been somewhat remiss in keeping his journal and is now making his half yearly report. Our Mr. Baltrop visited the boy on April 5. No special notes. Letters were received from Curling's employers on May 12 and June 23. A letter was received from the boy on May 22. The above letters from employers refer to the transfer of this boy from situation to situation. Mr. Storey returned the boy to us on April 12. Curling was then sent to a Mr. John Jones of Randwhich on

April 14. On May 13 Mr. Jones reports that the boy is very untruthful, chews tobacco when he can get it and uses bad language. Mr. Jones thinks it will be a difficult matter to make a good boy out of him. Curling was returned by this gentleman for insolence and laziness on May 13 and sent on the same day to Mr. John Fifer, a farmer living at Richard's Landing, St. Joseph's Island. In the two letters we have received from Mr. Fifer since taking the boy, we are informed that the boy arrived safely, is happy, and likes his place. But, according to his employer, he does not work unless watched and is otherwise not altogether giving satisfaction. The terms of our agreement with Mr. Fifer are 20 dollars for the current year with board and lodging. On May 27, Mr. Owen, of our staff, sent the boy a letter advising him to turn over a new leaf.

February 21, 1891 (Fred is 15 and a half years old) Again Mr. Owens submits a half yearly report. We received a letter from Mr. Fifer on September 22. The contents of the letter were very disturbing. Mr. Fifer notes that the boy is very untruthful and will not work unless under close supervision. This boy has also, on more than one occasion, attempted to commit an indecent assault on Mr. Fifer's little girl. She is just 7 years of age. On September 23 we wrote in reply expressing our deep regret and advising Mr. Fifer what steps to take in the event of the repetition of any such offense. This to include the use of severe corporal punishment. We have heard nothing further but from the boy's previous record, we fear that he is not likely to turn out in any way satisfactory.

July 1, 1891 (Fred is 16 years old now) Owen's half year report. We received a letter from Frederick on May 7 indicating that he was leaving Mr. Fifer to enter into employment with a Mr. Rouse. The local storekeeper in Richard's Landing informs us that Mr. Rouse is a good, honest and respectable man. Frederick has grown to be stout and strong and should be capable of a great deal of useful work. However, his employers do not see that in his actions. Mr. Fifer indicates that Curling is "a terrible boy" and cannot be trusted out of sight. He goes on to say that Curling has given him a great deal of trouble. He says that the boy abuses the cattle and children and has got acquainted with very low people who do not advise him for his good. Mr. Fifer further states that on one occasion Curling was punished for sucking eggs and threatened to stab Mr. Fifer. We cannot say how far this is the cause but we fear that there is at any rate some grounds for complaint. On the 14th of May Curling was transferred from John Fifer to Leonard Rouse of Richards Landing, with whom the lad has a thoroughly respectable farm home. He has been engaged at a rate of thirty dollars per year, with board and lodging.

February 1, 1892 (Fred is 16 and a half years old) Mr. Owens submits another half year report. He states that no information has been received regarding Frederick. His address is still in care of Mr. Levi Rouse of Richard's Landing.

Frederick Curling would have been nearly seventeen years old at this point and would have been capable of going out on his own. Unfortunately, Barnardos has no other direct contact with him and the trail is lost. Until he pops up in the lives of his nieces, Alice Maud and Florence Gertrude, and nephew Albert.

From other sources we learn that the 1901 census taken in England lists a Frederick Curling. This person was two years old and the son of James Curling (aged 28), and Mary Curling. They all lived at 47 Griffith Street, civil parish St. Paul, parliamentary borough Deptford. Very likely this child was the nephew of our Frederick Curling, the brother of James Curling who was spared the life of a Barnardo child. Unfortunately, that life seemed destined for James' son.

At age 12 Frederick, the son of James Curling, went to Canada as the youngest of fourteen children from Barnardos. He eventually went to Sioux, Michigan, married and had eight children. All of them, except the youngest, were born in the United States. The children of this union are as follows: Blanche (oldest), May (who married Lloyd Small and had no children), Gladys (she and her husband were killed in Florida and had

40

no children), Howard (he moved to Vancouver), Edna (maybe this is Blanche) married Ed Durnan and they had three children, and Florence who married William Neikel and had two sons, last known to be living in Richmond Hill. This phone number was given as a contact: 905 884 3007. Diane Kirby actually called this number and spoke with a woman who was not able to provide much information other than that she had a brother who also lived there. Diane hopes that the woman's brother will call to talk about the family.

Alice Maud Jackson

Alice was Born April 8, 1889, second child, and second daughter, to Albert Jackson and Ellen Curling Jackson. At the age of nine, she entered Barnardo's on July 12, 1898 and was sent to the girls cottage village in Ilford, England where she lived in Wild Thyme cottage. She was of the Anglican faith.

Her mother Ellen Curling Jackson was very much against her two girls being sent to Canada and asked for their restoration to her home. Emigration had received a letter stating that Ellen Curling Jackson was a woman of good character so they postponed movement of the girls from her home until an investigation was done. On July 17, 1901 the mother's application for restoration was declined. The investigation reveals that although she is a good woman, it is clearly not a case for restoration and it would be well to consider it for emigration.

At the age of twelve, Alice Maud left Liverpool, England, bound for Canada. She departed on September 19, 1901 onboard the SS Tunisian and arrived in Peterborough, Ontario on September 27. She and her sister Gertrude Florence sailed together as part of a group of 105 Barnardo girls. They remained in Peterborough awaiting their assignment to a new home, and new life in Canada.

October 14, 1901 (Alice is 12 years old) Ellen Curling Jackson receives a letter stating that both girls had arrived safely in Canada. A photograph of them is enclosed.

October 18   Ellen Curling Jackson sends us a letter of thanks stating that she is sorry that the girls have left, but indicating that she will be coming to Canada to see for herself their situation in the spring.

November 22   Alice is sent to live with Mrs. William Forrest who resides in Hoards Station. Mr. Forrest is a farmer.

December 11   We received a letter from Mrs. Forrest. She says that she likes Alice so far, and that the girl is going to school.

December 15   We sent a letter to Alice. No copy was kept.

December 28   We received a letter from Alice. She says she is very happy.

January 18, 1902 (Alice is almost 13 years old)   We received a letter from Alice. She states no complaints and indicates that she is happy and kindly treated. She is attending the Methodist church and Sunday school as well as daily school. Her current home is about three miles from her sister Florence Gertrude.

Florence & Alice Jackson 1898

September 10 We received a letter from Mrs. Forrest. She states that the girl is unsatisfactory. No specifics given.

September 20 We sent a letter to Mrs. Forrest asking her about the condition of Alice's clothing.

September 24 In a letter received from Mrs. Forrest today, she says that she will keep Alice for now.

October 24 Today we received a letter from Mrs. Forrest stating that the girl is useless. Mrs. Forrest has given notice that Alice must leave.

November 7 On this date we have transferred Alice from Mrs. Forrest to a Mrs. Thomas E. Hooper of Menie, Ontario.

November 10 We received a letter from Mrs. Hooper stating that Alice had arrived and was in a safe arrangement.

December 24 Todays letter from Mrs. Hooper states that she is sending Alice back to us. The girl is so slow and useless to her.

December 29 Another letter from Mrs. Hooper. She has changed her mind and will keep Alice. She has withdrawn her notice of termination.

January 8, 1903 (Alice is 13 years old)
Alice was visited by our Miss Gibbs today. Her health is good and she looks well. Miss Gibbs confirms Mrs. Hooper's comments about Alice

being slow and adds that the girl is slovenly and careless, tends to be easygoing and is evidently not fond of work.

February 3   Our office has received a letter from Alice's mother asking for the address of Florence, Alice's sister.

February 5   We sent a letter to the mother giving her the address of our home in Canada and telling her that according to the latest reports, Florence was doing well.

February 13   We received a letter from the girl's mother demanding the actual address where Florence is Living, and not that of our Canadian home.

April 29   We received a letter from Mrs. Hooper today. She states that she will be sending Alice back to us in May.

May 9   We received a letter today from Mrs. Hooper authorizing us to transfer Alice to the home of a Mrs. R. A. Linn, also of Menie.

June 6   We received a letter today letter from Mrs. Linn indicating that Alice had arrived.

July 30   On this day we received a letter from Alice. (no specifics of letter's contents)

December 9   Alice and Mrs. Linn were visited by our Miss Poole today. She defines Alice as a fair, refined girl, gentle and good looking, but a girl who will not work properly. Miss Poole is not satisfied with this placement for this girl. This home would be better for a rougher girl but Alice wants to stay another year. The girl cannot write vey well so she would like to attend three months of school. She is attending the Presbyterian church and Sunday school and should go to school during January, February and March.

January 20, 1904 (Alice is 14 years old)   We received a letter from Mrs. Linn today agreeing to send the girl to school.

May 27   A letter arrived from England today addressed to Alice. It was postmarked Forest Hill, S O and was forwarded to the girl. (There is no indication of who the letter was from or what its contents were. It could have come from one of several places in England: Forest Hill, Southern Oxfordshire, an ancient village near the city of Oxford; or from Forest Hill, a village southeast of London.)

July 22   We received a letter from Alice's mother inquiring about the girl. (Notation in the records says see reply and letter to girl but makes no comments as to nature of reply.)

November 12 Alice was visited by Miss Gibbs today. Miss Gibbs notes that the girl is well provided for in clothing.

November 22 We received a letter from Mrs. Linn complaining that the girl is very incompetent.

During the **period November 22, 1904 through October 14, 1905** there is an exchange of letters between our office and Mrs. Linn regarding the amount she is paying for the employment of the girl and how much she receives to care for the girl. Mrs. Linn feels she is paying very well for little received and has done a lot of sewing for the girl and has not charged much. In the end, she sends Alice back to us.

October 12, 1905 (Alice is now 16 years old)
Our office has received a letter from William Owen in England indicating that the Royal Family, in particular Queen Alexandra , wife of Edward VII who became King Of England upon the death of Queen Victoria in 1901, has taken a personal interest in this child and her sister Florence because the girl's mother has petitioned for their return. Please watch carefully are the instructions.

Queen Alexandra may have become interested in these children because she herself was no stranger to misfortune. Although royal, she was the daughter of the King and Queen of Denmark, she was not raised in luxury. And, she was born with an hereditary condition which caused her to become increasingly deaf, and socially ostracized, as she grew older.

November 6 Mrs. Linn informs us through a letter that she is refusing to send the girl back until April, saying this was her agreement.

November 9 We replied to Mrs. Linn with a letter stating that we must insist that she return the girl to us as we have requested.

November 18 Alice was visited by our Mrs. Reazin today. Alice appears to be a healthy, neat, clean, quiet, and nice girl. She does not attend church or Sunday school. Mrs. Reazin indicates that the girl is very unhappy and wishes to leave this situation. Alice complains that she works hard, goes nowhere, and that the mistress does not use her at all kindly. Mrs. Reazin found Alice alone and working hard. Mrs. Reazin agrees to let Mrs. Linn keep Alice until April, at the price Mrs. Linn insists on. Alice is very unhappy and wants to leave.

November 20 We have decided to overrule Mrs. Reazin's decision to allow Mrs. Linn to keep Alice until April and have written a letter to Mrs. Linn indicating that she must return the girl to us by November 30 of this year.

November 30 Alice returns to us in order that she might be placed closer to her sister Florence.

At this time we find her to be a small pleasant girl, rather slow and quiet, neatly dressed. She says that she was lonely with Mrs. Linn, but not unkindly treated.

December 1905   Alice is sent to Mrs. J. Monk of Springford, where she will live and work on the Monk's farm. Alice sends us a letter indicating that she likes the Monk's home, and a letter from her mother is forwarded to her,

February 1906   We have sent a letter to Mrs. Monk asking how the girl is getting on.

March 1906   We have received a letter from Mrs. Monk in which she indicates that the girl is quiet and pleasant, but self willed and unsettled by the letter from her mother. Mrs. Monk concludes that she is not sure if Alice will be sufficient help for summer work.

March 1906 (Alice will be 17 years old next month)   We sent a letter to Mrs. Monk regretting to hear this news. The subject was left open and it is hoped that Alice will be able to remain with Mrs. Monk.

July 16   We have sent a report to our offices in Stepney, England regarding both girls. Alice was moved by arrangement to a place (Monk family) closer to her sister Florence after complaining that she was lonely in her former house.

Florence is living in a nice farmhouse where she is happy.

August 10   We are arranging for a visit to check on the girls.

August 13 Alice was visited by Mrs. Gibbs. This was a special visit based on a letter from England inquiring of the girl (author not specified). Mrs. Gibbs says she does not feel satisfied about the girl's surroundings and two weeks notice to leave was given to the mistress. Alice does not seem very happy but Mrs. Gibbs fears that she is inclined to feel morbid and discontented. Alice is a good deal unsettled by letters from her mother who wants to get the girls home and Alice has no doubt set her mind on this. She has lately felt troubled because she has not received an answer to her last letter written to her mother in February. Mrs. Monk complains Alice is slow and not much help. Alice feels she is kept close at work, would rather be doing something like sewing than housework. A letter was sent to Mrs. Monk arranging the journey for the girl to return and she returned to us.

August 26   Alice comes back to us at Hazelbrea (the home that Barnardo used as his girl's distribution center outside of Peterborough, Ontario.)

September   Alice was sent to Mrs. G. R. Michie, of Lindsay. This is a temporary arrangement as Mrs. Michie is moving to Port Arthur and will not be able to take the girl with her.

September 20 Mrs. Michie writes to say that she finds the girl slow but likes her disposition and asks if her wages can be lowered for the first six months of our agreement.

October Alice is moved to Mrs. Sylvester in Lindsay. Another temporary arrangement.

November A woman named Mrs. Lynch telephoned our office to ask if Alice could go to a Catholic family, indicating that Mrs. Sylvester had agreed to this. Mrs. Lynch was told that such an arrangement could not possibly be allowed and that Mrs. Sylvester would be contacted in regard to this.

We sent a strong letter to Mrs. Sylvester stating that under no circumstances could the girl go to a Catholic family and that if she no longer wanted the girl, she must be returned to us here.

December We have forwarded two letters to Alice from her mother.

December Alice was visited by Mrs. Reazin. (No details of this visit were recorded.)

February 5, 1907 (Alice is nearly 18 years old) Another letter was sent to Mrs. Sylvester today stating that we had received a report that she had sold Alice a second hand coat. She was informed that this was not permitted as we do not allow mistresses to sell children clothing. We told her that the child must be reimbursed the cost of coat.

April 15 (There is an odd jump in the records here. Somewhere Alice went from Mrs. Sylvester to a Mrs. Warner, but this movement is not noted in the records.) Mrs. Reazin writes to Alice saying she should give Mrs. Warner (?) notice that she will be leaving. Alice replies that Mrs. Warner has been so kind she doesn't know how to broach the subject. Alice says she would like to remain with Mrs. Warner, but Mrs. Reazin says that it would not be in her best interest to do so. (No explanation of this reasoning is given.)

April 16 We sent a letter to Mrs. Reazin advising her that we are giving notice to Mrs. Warner.

April 22 We received a letter from Mrs. Strong asking to send the girl to her around the first of May.

April 29 Alice returns to us.

April 30   Alice is placed with Mrs. Frank P Strong of Bolborne.

May 2   We sent a letter to Mrs. Strong with our hope that Alice has arrived safely.

May 4   Alice writes of her safe journey and to report that she is pleased with her new home. She also asks that Florence be found a new place.

July 10   The girl's mother, Ellen Curling Jackson, has again written to our office. She is demanding to know Alice's address. We sent a reply giving her the last address we have on file for Alice.

August 5   Alice has been transferred to Mrs. G. E. R. Wilson, drawer 266, Colborne, Ontario.

October 11   Alice is visited by Mrs. Reazin. The girl is described as a healthy good-sized girl, rather nice in appearance. She goes on to say that Alice is getting along well, is highly spoken of, and is quite content where she is.

November 4   Mrs. Reazin again visits Alice. She is in good health, and has become a capable maid. She is very thorough and clean about her work. She has an excellent house and has been on a recent visit to Toronto to see her mother. The mother talks of returning to England and taking Alice with her, but Alice doesn't want to leave the Wilsons. She is attending the Church of England.

September 16, 1909 (Alice would be approaching her 21st birthday) Mrs. Reazin reports that Alice went to Toronto five weeks ago to see her mother. Her return to Mrs. Wilson is uncertain. She had a good reputation in the village of Balbourne.

Alice Maud is believed to have immigrated to the United States in 1921. She and her oldest sister, Nellie, are thought to have lived and worked on a farm somewhere along the way as they moved to settle in Santa Monica, California.

Records from the 1930 US census indicate that Alice was single, aged 40, and had never married. She was unemployed but worked as a private nurse and lived in a rooming house at 1617 Ocean Avenue, Santa Monica, California.

June 25, 1932 (Alice would be 43 now) We have heard that Alice can now be reached in care of a Mrs. Brooks, 1390 Appleton Way, Venice, California, United States. (Francis Rose, Alice's youngest sister, would have been a Mrs. Brooks who lived in Venice at this time).

Florence Gertrude Jackson

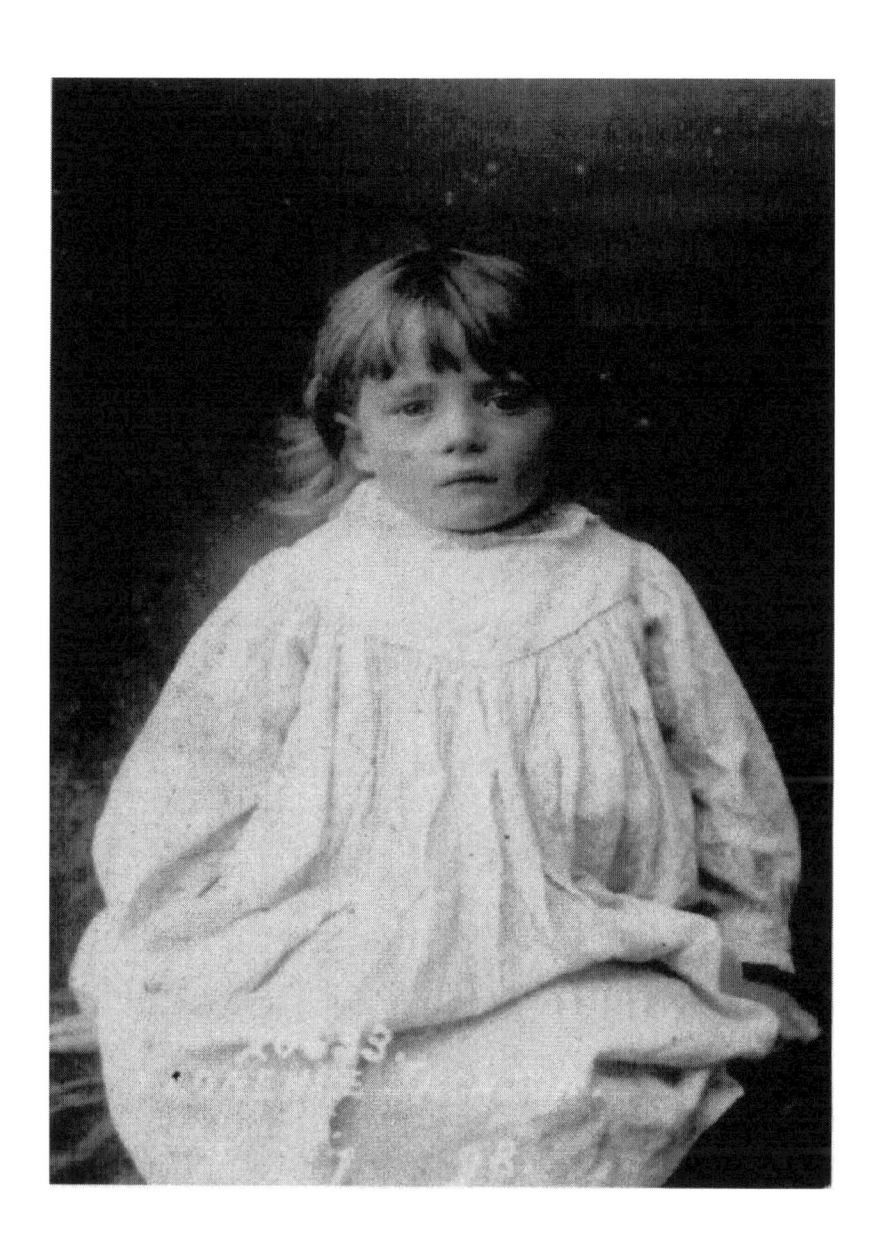

Florence Gertrude Jackson was born February 23, 1893, in Brockley, South London. She was the fourth child and third daughter of Albert Jackson and Ellen Curling Jackson.

At the tender age of five years and four months, Florence Gertrude was admitted to Barnardo's on July 12, 1898. She spent three nights at the Stepney receiving home before being sent to the Girls Village Cottages in Ilford, England where she resided in the Wild Thyme cottage.

She remained in Ilford until 1901 when on September 19, she and a group of 104 other Barnardo girls, including her sister Alice, sailed aboard the SS Tunisian out of Liverpool for Canada. They most likely would have sailed down the St. Lawrence River to Toronto, on Lake Ontario and then gone overland to their destination of Peterborough, Ontario on September 27. Here they would wait to be sent to begin a new life with a new Canadian "family."

October 1, 1901 (Florence Gertrude is 8 years old) Florence Gertrude was this day placed with a Mrs. James Watson of Burnbrae, a small town east of Peterborough.

November 7   Florence Gertrude indicates to us that she is being kindly treated at the home of Mrs. Watson, but adds that she wants to hear from her mother in England.

October 23, 1903 (Florence Gertrude is 10 years old)   Mrs. Watson has contacted our office and states that she would like to adopt Florence Gertrude. A big step indeed.

December 9   On a visit from one of our staff, Florence Gertrude is reported to be healthy. She is a pretty girl, her conduct is good on the whole, but she is inclined to answer back and is very hot tempered. The report goes on to say that she is very slow, unless she chooses not to be. This is one of the best homes that we have placed one of our girls with. The girl is happy, being well trained, and learning music. About this she is well pleased. She is attending church and Sunday school and day school, all of which is required and done. Florence Gertrude has contacted her mother and sees her sister Alice on occasion.

November 12, 1904 (Florence Gertrude is 11 years old)   One of our staff visited with Florence Gertrude and reports that she is a pleasant looking girl but not particularly bright. The home is neat and clean with two little children. The mistress did make a complaint against her about stealing cakes from the cellar. The girl herself is discontented, as her mistress is inclined to be a little sharp. But the mistress is probably tired by the girl's slow ways. Florence Gertrude is small for her age with pretty, long, fair hair and inclined to be a little saucy. Apparently she is not very obedient. This child has a good home and is inclined to presume on her privileges. If she is good, Mrs. Watson is willing to keep her after payment ceases.

May 15, 1905 (Florence Gertrude is 12 years old) We have received a letter from Mrs. Watson complaining that the girl is self willed, disobedient and must leave. She also indicates that the girl's mother has written to the daughter and the letters are very unsettling to the girl. Out of our frustration we have written to Mrs. Jackson to tell her that she can take the girl home if she likes.

May 16   We have sent a letter to Mrs. Watson regretting the trouble caused by the girl's Mother. We have also sent a letter to Florence Gertrude urging improvement in her behavior and demeanor, for her own good.

September 7   Mrs. Watson has written to us to return the girl. We have agreed to take her back.

September 27   The girl returned to us today. She is a fair, delicately looking child, nicely dressed.

September 28   Florence Gertrude was sent to the home of a Mrs. George Parsons of Otterville.

October 12   We have received word from our offices in England that the girls' mother, Ellen Curling Jackson, has filed a complaint with Queen Alexandra (wife of Edward VII). Her Highness has taken a personal interest in this child. We are advised to keep a close eye on the situation.

November 22   Reports to our office indicate that the Parsons' home is a good farmhouse with four children. Florence Gertrude is a bright little girl, good tempered, and works well. She attends church and Sunday school, takes school lessons at home, and is working in the 4th book. Gertrude is wanting very much in manners. She has a good home which she likes very much and is well cared for.

August 3, 1906 (Florence Gertrude is 13 years old) On a visit from our staff, Mrs. Parsons tells us that she is not altogether satisfied with the girl. Mrs. Parsons says Florence Gertrude looks too much of a child and complains that the girl is slow, idle, careless and dirty about herself. She neglects herself. Our visitor found the girl to be a bright, intelligent child with a good disposition.

August 27   Florence Gertrude returned to us today. Her former mistress, Mrs. Parsons, determined that the girl was too small for her needs.

September 6   Florence Gertrude has this day been placed with Mrs. Charles Lindsay of 45 Cambridge Street, Lindsay, Ontario. This is a nice comfortable place. Mrs. Lindsay is a pleasant young woman with a baby.

October 15   Mrs. Lindsay has contacted us to complain of the girl's carelessness and want of personal cleanliness.

December 12   On our recent visit we found that the girl has a private room in a good home. However, her mistress indicates that her conduct has been not at all satisfactory. She states that the girl is deceitful, untruthful, and overall of very little use. She further states that she will not keep the girl unless she improves. Mrs. Lindsay thinks Alice is a bad influence and the two should be further apart.

February 22, 1907 (Tomorrow Florence Gertrude will be 14)   Mrs. Lindsay has asked that the girl be exchanged.

March 8   Mrs. Lindsay has agreed that she will keep the girl for another month. Primarily because we have told her that no other girl will be available for her home until June.

May 4   Alice Jackson, sister of Florence Gertrude, has written to our office asking for a place where Florence Gertrude can go to school indicating that Florence Gertrude has not been to school since she was twelve years old. That would have been nearly two years ago. She further states that her sister is not being used properly by her mistress.

June 24   We received a postcard from Florence Gertrude asking for her sister Alice's address.

June 27   Mrs. Lindsay has written to say that she must part with Florence Gertrude and is asking when can she expect another boarder.

June 28   We have learned that Frederick Curling, uncle to Alice and Florence Gertrude, is living in Sault Saint Marie and is a most disturbing element in the lives of both girls. This is because he has been in contact with them asking them to join him where he is. Alice plans to join him in August and Florence Gertrude wants to join them. Mrs. Lindsay continues to complain of the girl's unsatisfactory behavior and has added that she will not keep her any longer. The girl does not even try to improve.

July 8   We have this day received a very unusual, and anonymous letter in regard to Florence Gertrude. The writer indicates that the girl is ill used, improperly fed, always late for church and Sunday school, and altogether very unhappy. The anonymous author of the letter has requested an investigation. (This may very well have been Alice writing the letter, or even Florence Gertrude herself!)

July 8   Florence Gertrude has returned to us once again.

July 12   Before placing this girl with another household, we have questioned her about her tenure at the Lindsay home. She told us that nothing was wrong and that she certainly doesn't know who wrote the mysterious and anonymous letter we received.

July 13   Florence Gertrude has been placed in the home of Mrs. Robert M. Hay of Campbellford. They live in a brick house that is well furnished and very comfortable.

July 17   We have received two messages today regarding Florence Gertrude. The first is a postcard from the girl stating that she likes the place and is not at all lonely. The second is a postcard from Mrs. Hay. She is thankful to us for sending her such a nice girl.

December 24   Florence Gertrude's sister Alice has contacted our office to get her sister's new address in order that she might go visit. We have learned that the girls' mother will be coming soon to Canada. She has inquired if Florence Gertrude could be handed over to her. The mother thinks the girl should be attending school. We will consider the advantages of handing the girl over to her mother. We have also sent a letter to Alice with a report on her sister's well being, and including her new address.

January 1, 1908 (Florence Gertrude is almost 15 years old)   We have learned that Florence Gertrude's mother and sisters are definitely coming to Canada from England. The girl is very happy about this, but anxious to join her mother. Florence Gertrude is now reported to have good conduct and she is living in a good home. She is quite excited to hear that her mother and sisters were to have sailed from England on the 27th of December.   She is expected to leave Mrs. Hay to go to be with her mother almost at once. She was, however, told she could not do this without our consent.

January 17   We have received an inquiry from Alice regarding her sister Florence Gertrude. Their mother is now in Toronto living at 11 Gerrard Place.

January 27   Ellen Curling Jackson, the girls mother, has sent a letter stating that she plans to come to our offices to visit with Florence Gertrude.

January 28   We have sent a letter to the mother indicating that the girl has a good home in Toronto and that we feel it would be unwise to disturb her.

March 27   One of our staff met Mrs. Jackson here today on her way to visit Florence Gertrude. She indicates that she may return to England. She would like to start a small store, perhaps here or in England. She was described as a tidy, well-mannered woman.

April 22   Mrs. Hay has contacted us to say that she no longer requires the girl. She states that her sister, Mrs. Rutherford, would like to engage the girl.

April 23   Florence Gertrude has gone to live with Mrs. Rutherford.

October 7   Our latest report indicates that the girl seems happy and is doing well.

October 16   Mrs. Rutherford has this day given notice to return the girl. We wrote to her inquiring as to the reason, stating that we trust that the mother has not been a disturbing element.

October 22   We have received a request from a Mrs. Mckelvie who states that she wants the girl.

November 5   In contacting Mrs. Rutherford, we have found that she speaks highly of the McKelvie home and states that the girl will have "as much care as we should give her". On this date we send Florence Gertrude to live with Jessie McKelvie, wife of John McKelvie who is a farmer in Campbellford.

January 11, 1909 (Florence Gertrude is almost 16 years old) We have heard that Florence Gertrude is very anxious to join her mother in Toronto.

January 11 We understand that the girl's conduct is good, that she speaks well of her home and mistress, but also asks to go to Toronto so she can see her mother sometimes. Florence Gertrude is attending the Presbyterian Church.

January 20 We have sent Florence Gertrude a letter advising her against joining her mother. She will be better off with the McKelvie family.

November 30, 1910 (Florence Gertrude is now 17 years old) Florence Gertrude left the McKelvie home more than a year ago. She went to Toronto to be with her mother. We do not have an address for her in Toronto.

1914 (Florence Gertrude is twenty one years old) We have located Ellen Curling Jackson in Toronto living at 672 Dupont Street.

1922 September (Florence Gertrude is 29 years old) We have heard that Florence

Gertrude is married to a Mr. Fred Kilby. They are living at 663 Balliol Street in Toronto.

1940 (Florence Gertrude is now 47 years old)
We learned this year that the girl's brother Albert had a tumor and is not expected to recover from a major operation. We also received a letter from Florence Gertrude inquiring of any information regarding her mother and any particulars of her parentage.

The Canadian branch of Barnardo's forwarded the request on to the main offices in England asking for the confidential history of the case. What transpired through a series of short letters was a bureaucratic mess. The branch in England wrote back saying that the last thing they knew about the mother was that in 1907 she contacted them inquiring about Florence Gertrude. And in 1941 they sent a letter to the 1907 address. Which was returned as "Not Known." Concluding that the mother was no longer there, and that any other relatives would be very old and unlikely to reply, the London office declared that no further effort would be made to locate the mother. They couldn't just send the info they had in their records. There was a war on.

Florence Gertrude married Fred Kilby on June 29, 1919, and together they had three daughters. They were Doris Lillian (April 6, 1920), Marjorie (Marge) (August 21 1921), and Thelma.

Florence Gertrude Jackson Kilby and her husband Fred Kilby

Fred Kilby was born in 1886 in England and immigrated to Canada in 1887 with his family. He was the son of Daniel and Emma Kilby. Both parents were born in England, Daniel on November 17, 1849 and Emma on March 6, 1853. Daniel was a teamster. Together they had six children, Frederick being the second to youngest. His siblings were Daniel C. (b. 1875), William R. (b. 1878), Harrietta (b. 1880), Florie (b. 1884) and Ellen G. (b. 1889). In 1901 the family lived at 167 Carlaw Avenue, Toronto. Mother and father, Daniel and Emma, are buried at Mount Pleasant Cemetery in Toronto.

Florence Gertrude's husband Fred Kilby worked for the United Typewriter Company as a pressman (per 1928 data) and lived with Florence Gertrude at 663 Balliol Street in Toronto. Here they raised their three daughters Doris, Marge and Thelma.

They later moved to 390 Balliol Street. This was the new home of their daughter Doris Kilby and her husband Edmund Turgeon who were married in 1939. Shortly after the wedding, Edmund went overseas to fight in World War Two. He was gone until 1945. During his absence, the whole family moved in with Doris including Florence Gertrude and Fred, Marge and Thelma. Florence Gertrude and Fred helped care for their first grandchild, Diane, who was the new-born daughter of Doris and Edmund. Diane was born after her father Edmund had gone overseas and they never saw each other until his return when she was five and a half years old. At the same time, Doris, Marge and Thelma were all working.

It was here that Fred Kilby died on December 11, 1944. The cause of death was listed as a cerebral hemorrhage. He was 59 years old and was buried in Mount Pleasant Cemetery in Toronto.

When Edmund returned from the war in 1945 he wanted to have the house for his family so Florence Gertrude and her two daughters, Marge and Thelma, left the house. Florence Gertrude and Thelma went to California to visit Florence Gertrude's mother, Ellen Curling Jackson, and sister Alice Maud.

Florence Gertrude returned to Toronto and went to work as a practical nurse. Eventually she was in the employ of a Mr. Rudolph Lembke as a housekeeper. Florence Gertrude and Rudolph "Rudy" Lembke were married in 1949.

Rudy is believed to have been born in 1881. His first wife was named Jane and she died in 1949 at the age of 69 years. Together Florence Gertrude and Rudy lived at 134 Duvernet Avenue on Toronto until they moved to Norland, Ontario. Rudolph died on November 4, 1966 at the age of 85. The cause of death was listed as chronic pyelonephritis or kidney failure. He is buried at Mount Pleasant Cemetery, Toronto.

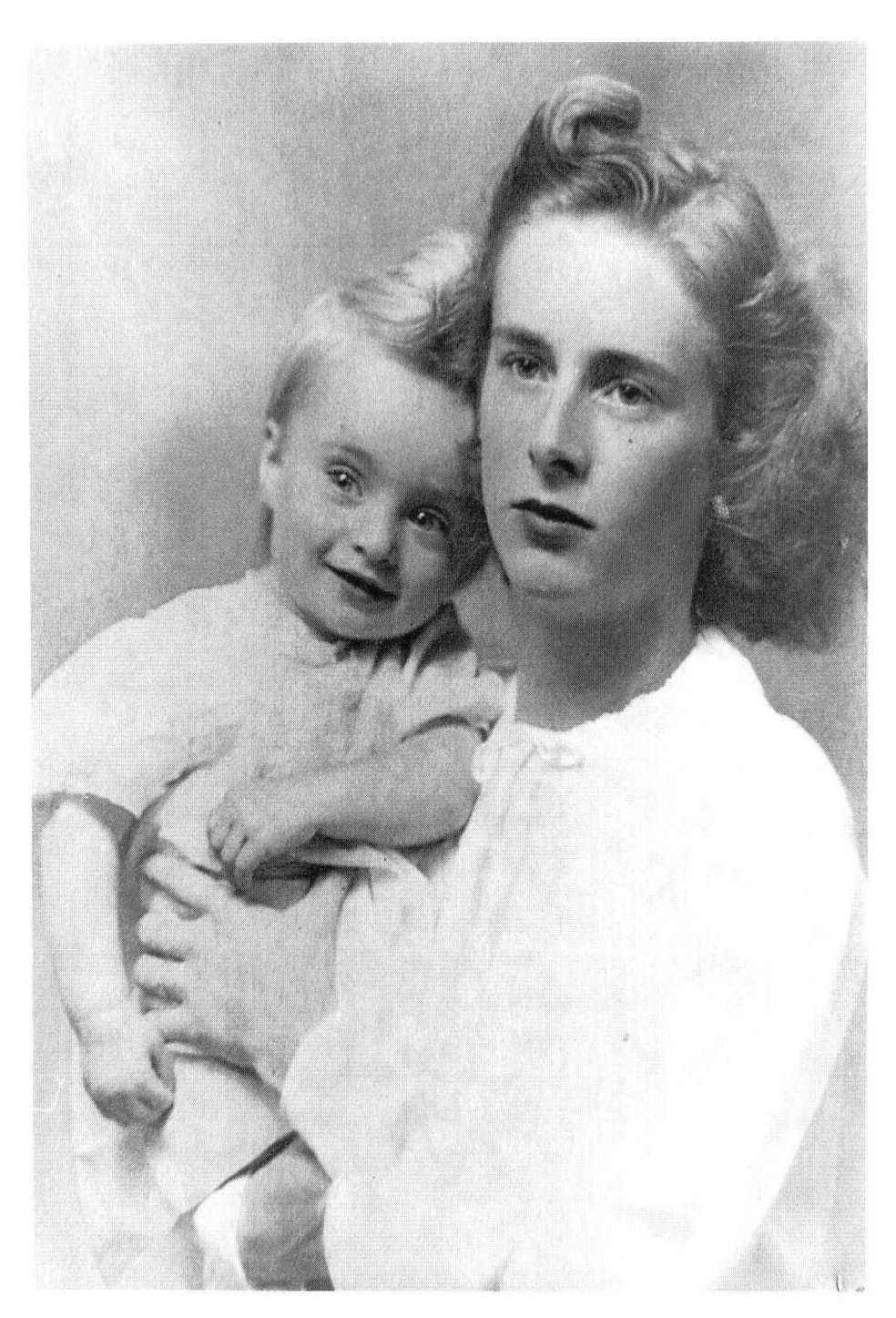

Doris Kilby and her daughter Diane

Doris, Thelma and Diane at 390 Balliol Street in Toronto

Florence Kilby later in life

Rudolph "Rudy" Lembke

Florence Gertrude herself remained in Norland until her death in 1975. She did not like hospitals and thought people went there to die. One day she wasn't feeling well and her daughter Marge convinced her to go to the Richmond Hill Hospital for a checkup. While Marge was waiting for the results of Florence Gertrude's exam, the Doctor came out and told her that her mother had passed away. Florence Gertrude had walked in, lay down and died! She was 82 years old. What a world she had seen.

Albert William Jackson

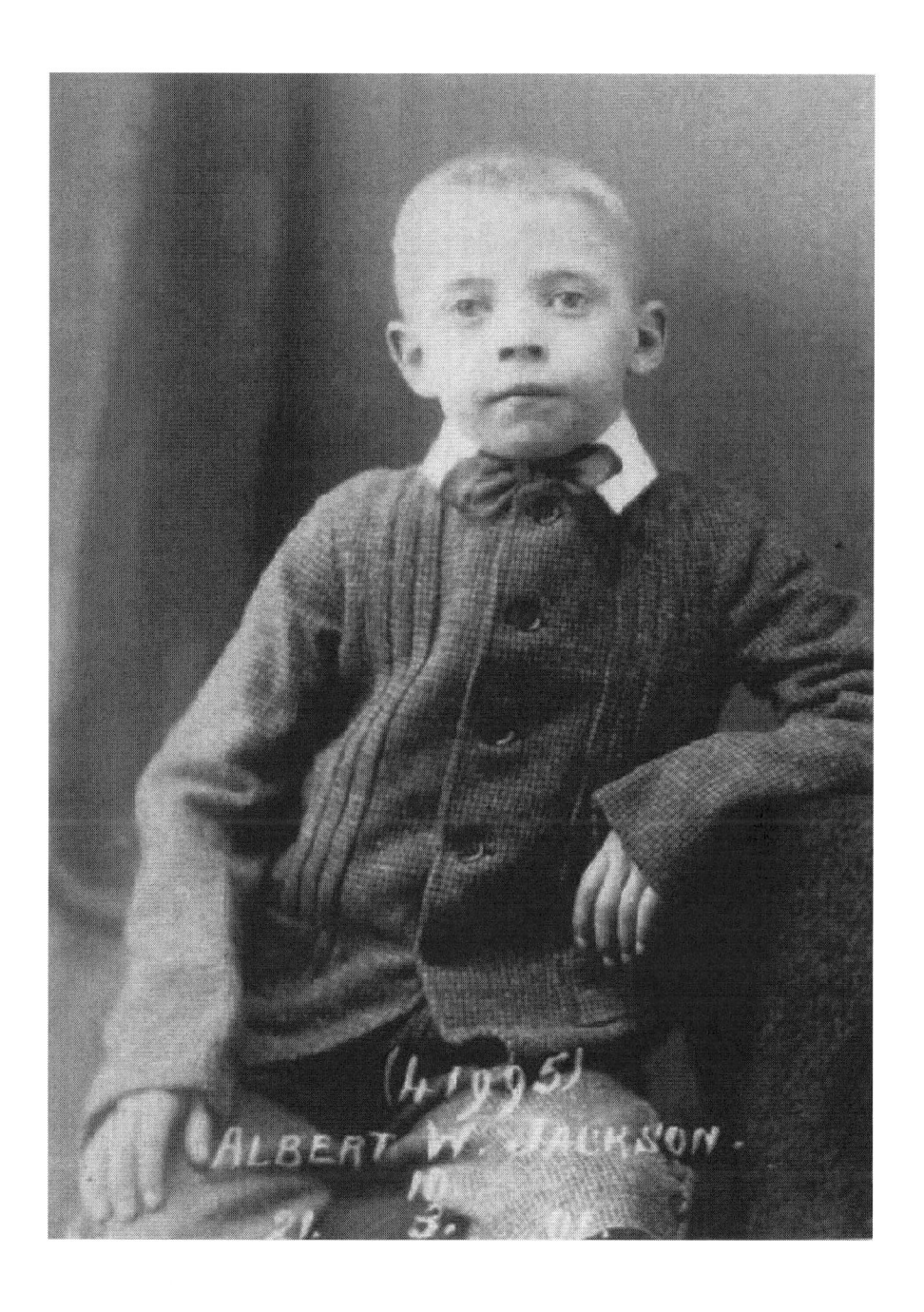

Albert William Jackson was born on April 12, 1891 at Deptford, South London. He was the second child, and only son, born to Albert Jackson and Ellen Curling Jackson. At the age of seven years and three months Albert was admitted to Barnardo's on July 12, 1898 with his two sisters Florence and Alice. He was described on his intake documents as being fair-haired, blue eyed, with a fair complexion. The Medical Officer states that Albert has a laryngeal obstruction. No notes on weight, chest size, or body condition were made.

Upon his admission he spent six nights at the receiving house in Stepney, East London and was then transferred to Sheppard House, also in East London. He remained at Sheppard House until November 1, 1898 when he went to live in Teighmore, Jersey, Channel Islands. On March 21 of 1901 Albert sailed from Liverpool, England aboard the SS Tunisian with 259 other Barnardo children for his new life in Canada. He arrived in Portland in Eastern Ontario on the Big Rideau Lake on March 30, 1901, went on to the Barnardo facility in Peterborough and began his Canadian journey.

April 2, 1901 (Albert is almost 10 years old now) Albert has been placed with Mr. Fred G. Haynes of Port Stanley, Yarmouth.

April 4   We received a post card from Albert saying that he arrived safely and that he likes the place very much indeed.

April 15   A letter was received from our head office post marked Jersey (most likely from his previous home on the Channel Islands) and was forwarded to the boy.

April 29   A letter postmarked Eltham was received and forwarded to Albert. (Author and contents unknown).

October 8   A letter was received from Albert's mother in England telling him that his uncle, Frederick Curling, lives in Richards Landing, St. Joseph's Island. The letter was forwarded to the boy.

October 25   Albert has written to our office enclosing a money order that he received from his mother. He says he will be glad if we will exchange the money order for him.

October 28   Another letter postmarked Eltham was received and forwarded to the boy. (Author and contents unknown). With that letter we sent our own letter with his money from the money order. We asked him to tell his mother that in the future it would be best to make money orders payable at Port Stanley to save time and postage.

January 21, 1902 (Albert is 10 years old)
Our office sent a letter to Mr. Haynes with the agreement regarding Albert for Mr. Haynes' signature.

January 29   Received a letter from Mr. Haynes with signed agreement.

March 10   Albert was visited by our Mr. Griffeth. He filed report number 16527. (Report not included with documents from Barnardo's)

June 10   A letter was received from Campbellford, Ontario addressed to Albert. We forwarded accordingly. (Author and contents unknown).

April 6, 1903 (Albert is almost 12 years old)
Today we received a letter from one of our young men named Fred L. Slade (103). He says that he and Albert Jackson are together and that they are chums.

April 27   Albert is visited by Mr. Griffith once again. Mr. Griffith filed report 19008 (copy of report not included in documents from Barnardo's)

February 13, 1904 (Albert is now almost 13 years old)   Mr. Haynes writes to us saying that the lad is of no use to him and he has decided to send him back to us next April. He also states that Albert is going to school at present.

February 13   We regrettably send a letter to Mr. Haynes accepting his notice to terminate Albert's employment.

March 20   Mr. Haynes writes to us that if we have not already found a place for the boy, Mr. Morley King of Kingsville would like to take the boy.

March 20   A letter is sent to Mr. Haynes enclosing an application for Mr. King to fill out regarding his request for the boy. Albert is returned to us this date.

April 5   Mr. Haynes writes to us enclosing a postal money order for the lad. Haynes says he would have sent it last week but was waiting for a reply to his letter.

April 8   Mr. Charles King writes to us enclosing his completed application to take on the boy. He goes on to explain that Morley King, as mentioned by Mr. Haynes, is his son so it is all the same if he himself sends the application as they live together in Kingsmill, Malahide Township.

April 16   Mr. Griffith of our staff reports that he saw Mr. Haynes and Haynes informed him that the lad shirked his work when possible, was untruthful and dishonest.   Griffith believes that Mr. Haynes is a sort of crank and although good in some ways, he is a man hard for a lad to get along with. At Haynes' home, the household bows down to him.

April 21   A letter is sent to Mr. King approving his application and proposing to send the boy to him around the 23rd of this month.

April 23   We have placed the boy with Mr. King this date.

April 29   We received a postcard from Albert saying that he arrived safely and likes his new place.

July 21   A letter was sent to Mr. King enclosing the agreement we have reached for his employment of Albert Jackson.

March 17, 1905 (Albert is now almost 14 years old)   After many months of not hearing from Mr. King, we sent a letter to him demanding that he immediately return the signed agreement for Albert's continued employment.

April 7   The signed agreement is finally received from Mr. King. No explanation of delay was received or noted.

June 23   We sent a letter to Albert showing him the present state of his account.

June 27   We received a letter from Albert inquiring as to why he isn't getting as much money this year as last. The answer, which was not relayed to him, is that his employment agreement this year, with Mr. King, stipulates a lower salary than the agreement with Mr. Haynes.

October 28   Albert was visited by our Mr. Griffith. Griffith submitted his report, number 26049. (Copy of report not included in documents from Barnardo's).

December 30   Albert has sent us his bankbook to have earned interest added to his records.

December 30   We sent a letter to Albert returning his bankbook with the account up to date through the end of this year.

April 9, 1906 (Albert is just shy of 15th birthday)   Albert has written to us stating that he has not yet received his bankbook from us.

April 13   We have sent a letter to Albert enclosing a new bankbook, up to date through the end of 1905.

April 24   We have received a letter, written by us to Albert, returned from the post office marked "not called for."

August   Albert was visited by our Mr. Griffith. Report number 29396 was submitted. (Copy of report not included in documents from Barnardo's).

December 21   A letter postmarked Lindsay was received here and forwarded to the boy. (This very likely was a letter from Albert's sister Alice who was living in Lindsay at the time.)

December 25   Albert writes saying that he has finally received his bankbook and that we have charged him for "Ups and Downs" for five years and he has only received it for two years. Ups and Downs was the quarterly newsletter coming from Barnardo's Canadian facilities and sent to each of the children placed.

December 27   We have written a letter to the boy saying that the Ups and Downs newsletters were sent to him, but on several occasions were returned through the post office dead letter file. We indicated that we don't want him to pay if he didn't receive the newsletter so we are crediting his account accordingly. We also enclosed a new bankbook and advised him that his account is being transferred to the Bank of Commerce.

February 8, 1907 (Albert is approaching his 16th birthday)   Albert has written acknowledging the receipt of his new bankbook and to tell us that he is getting along very well.

March 4   We have this day sent a letter to Mr. King advising him that our agreement regarding his employment of Albert Jackson expires on April 1. We have requested his payment for renewal of the agreement and are leaving the lad at liberty to make arrangements with Mr. King for his own hiring.

April 3   We received a letter from Mr. King enclosing the boy's wages and stating that the lad wishes to stay another year.

April 4   We sent a letter to Mr. King enclosing an official receipt for his payment and asking him to send lad's bankbook so that we may update the records.

April 9   Albert has sent us a letter enclosing his bankbook to be entered up.

August 17   Albert was visited by our Mr. Rogers who filed report 32690. (Copy of report not included in documents from Barnardo's).

October 8   Albert writes enclosing his bankbook and asking for a certain amount of money to be withdrawn from his account. He states that he has needs and of late Mr. king has refused to give him any more money until his time is out.

October 8   We have sent a letter to Albert enclosing the money that he had requested.

October 24   A silver medal is sent to the boy. (No notation as to what the medal is for.)

November 5   Albert writes to say he has not received the medal and is afraid that it has gone astray.

November 6   With concern for the disappearance of the boy's silver medal, we have asked the post office to make inquiry into it's whereabouts.

November 28   Albert writes to say that he has received the medal and is very pleased with it.

April 29, 1908 (Albert is 17 years old)
Albert called on our office in person today and withdrew ten dollars from his account. He tells us that he is now working with Keith and Fitzsimmons, plumbers in Kingsmill and is living with his mother at number 6, Seward Avenue, Toronto.

May 4   Albert withdraws another ten dollars from his account. He is still at the same address.

May 27   Albert withdraws another twenty dollars from his account. He says that he expects to go to Kingsmill Saturday where he has secured a job in a cheese factory earning twenty dollars per month and board.

October 3   Albert closes his bank account and states that he expects to go to Stalwart, Michigan. He is going to be with his Uncle Frederick in April.

May 27, 1909 (Albert is now 18 years old)
Albert has been missing since last fall. We believe he may be in Toronto.

April 29, 1910 (Hardly a boy, Albert is now 19 years old)   Mr. Kidner of our staff can only report that the boy is "out west". Believed to be in Carberry, Northwest Territory.

March 1911 Our staff files report 52761. (Copy of report not included in documents from Barnardo's).

November 7, 1911 (Albert is 20 years old)
Our staff files report 57822. (Copy of report not included in documents from Barnardo's).

No further entries regarding Albert.

From other sources it is known that Albert married a woman named Jessie and they eventually lived in Richmond Hill or Toronto. Together they had six children. They are Eleanor, Victoria (went to Texas), Ruth (youngest) who also went to Texas, Albert "Buster", Bob, and Ted who went to New York. Albert "Buster" Jackson died in Newmarket, north of Toronto, and is buried in the Elgin Mills Cemetery in Richmond Hill, Ontario.

Albert died at the age of 42 from a stomach tumor.

Rose and Nellie

Ellen Edith was the oldest, and Francis Rose the youngest of the Jackson children. "Nellie" was born in 1888 and Rose in 1894, both at 93 Childeric in Greenwich, Deptford, outside of London. This would have been a residential area of row houses about a mile from the river Thames and less than two miles from the Royal Observatory of Greenwich, the home of the zero longitude line.

When their father committed suicide these two stayed with their mother. Nellie, it was argued, was old enough at age ten that she could help her mother care for Rose, age four. This was to be especially true when Ellen Curling Jackson became ill shortly after her husbands death. The three middle children all went through the Barnardo system and were sent to Canada as Home Children in 1901.

Ellen, Nellie and Rose all left for Canada in 1907 to find the other three members of the family then in Canada. They sailed on the SS Britannia landing in Quebec City.

As these two girls were not involved in the Barnardo system, there are no records of them through Barnardo's. Thus, there is little record of them at all. There are some things known however.

Rose married a James Herbert Brooks. He was born in London on September 21, 1888, the son of Thomas Brooks and Eliza Gill. He and his sister Nancy came to Canada from London on board the SS Britannia, probably in 1901 and landed at Quebec City. He and Francis Rose were married on January 27, 1912 when he was age twenty-four and she age eighteen. This was the same day that Francis Rose became a Canadian citizen. James was then employed as a motorman. In 1914 the two of them were living at 672 DuPont Street in Toronto when he enlisted in the Canadian military to fight in World War One. While in France he was looked after by a Yvonne Douchet and her husband. In 1949 James was listed as a mechanic living at 79 Castlefield Avenue, Toronto.

Rose and James had four children. Winifred was born mostly likely in 1913. She died on July 30, 1984 in Vermont. Rose had a difficult birth with Winifred. The doctor even wanted to save Frances Rose at the cost of letting Winifred go but he ended up saving both. Winifred however, had scars on her head from the forceps used during her birth.

Ivy (Grace) was born and died in 1915. She rests in Prospect Cemetery, 1450 St. Clair Avenue West in Toronto.

Ellen curling Jackson and Her oldest daughter
Nellie

Kay (Kathleen Yvonne) was born on June 1, 1921. She died on September 28, 1977 and also rests in Prospect Cemetery.

Marg (Margaret) lives in Ottawa. She was born February 9, 1926 in Venice California. She lived there until she was seven years old.

James died on September 20, 1971. He was cremated and rests in Prospect Cemetery. Francis Rose died on January 27, 1986, the seventy-fourth anniversary of her marriage to James. Her final days were spent at Scarborough General Hospital where she died at age ninety-two. She was cremated and on February 3, 1986 was laid to rest in Prospect Cemetery.

Ellen Edith, nicknamed "Nellie" was the oldest of the five Jackson children. She was born in August of 1888. After sailing to Canada with their mother and sister Francis Rose in 1907, there is little information regarding her until 1918 and 1919 when we find that her first husband, name unknown, died of the terrible Spanish Flu epidemic that swept the world. Moving to California and possibly with Ellen, their mother, she married her second husband, a Mr. Jack Gates. They lived on Amarosa Street, or Amarosa Avenue, in Venice or Santa Monica, California. She and Jack had no children, but apparently she was more of a mother to Francis Rose's daughter Marg than was Francis Rose herself.

The Aftermath

By the end Barnardo had taken in 60,000 children and sent 20.000 to Canada. He even had a steamship where he trained boys for life in the Royal Navy. Like McPherson and Rye before him, his intentions were good. And he did his best to help these children. But were his actions really helpful?

There is no way of knowing how these tens of thousands of children would have turned out without his aid. Surely many would have died at an early age from exposure, starvation, neglect and abuse. But was Canada a better place for them?

The morality of the day included the notion that children were not fully formed human beings. That they needed to be beaten into shape. Even the bible said that beating a child wasn't necessarily bad for them. And with this frame of mind, Canadian society tried to take away any sense of self from the children.

The most progressive view of the day, in 1908, was the Ladies Home Journal view that children were not depraved and that raising children was a serious and involving task. Children actually had feelings. But it would still be 30 years or so before the field of child psychology was developed.

In 1909, South African-born Kingsley Fairbridge founded the "Society for the Furtherance of Child Emigration to the Colonies" which was later incorporated as the Child Emigration Society. The purpose of the society, which later became the Fairbridge Foundation, was to educate orphaned and neglected children and train them in farming practices at farm schools located throughout the British Empire. Fairbridge emigrated to Australia in 1912, where his ideas received support and encouragement. According to the British House of Commons Child Migrant's Trust Report, "it is estimated that some 150,000 children were dispatched over a period of 350 years—the earliest recorded child migrants left Britain for the Virginia Colony in 1618, and the process did not finally end until the late 1960s."

It was widely believed by contemporaries that all of these children were orphans, but it is now known that most had living parents, some of whom had no idea of the fate of their children after they were left in care homes, and some were led to believe that their children had been adopted somewhere in Britain.

Child emigration was suspended for economic reasons during the Great Depression of the 1930s but was not completely terminated until the 1970s.

As they were compulsorily shipped out of Britain, many of the children were deceived into believing their parents were dead, and that a more abundant life awaited them.

Some children were welcomed into loving homes, but others were exploited as cheap agricultural labor, or denied proper shelter and education and not allowed to socialize with native children. It was common for Home Children to run away, sometimes finding a caring family or better working conditions.

The rosy picture of Canada painted by those sending children to her shores were the images of life that the children expected to find there. There is anecdotal evidence suggesting that at least one young girl had just finished reading *Anne of Green Gables* when she was told she was going to Canada, and she was so excited to be going to this paradise.

The children were sent abroad and indentured until age 18 in exchange for food, clothing, and shelter, at least until the age 15 or 16 when they would start getting paid but would then have to begin to buy their own clothing.

Some of the situations that these children went to were the homes of well to do Canadians. Others were hardscrabble farms in remote areas where the farmers were poor, and the child, as a servant, was even poorer. They were often worked hard, abused, sexually assaulted and treated poorly. There are stories of children dying from neglect while in the custody of their Canadian rescuers. And there were stories of the children fighting back. And of others giving up and taking their own lives.

As we have seen through the eyes of the Jackson children who lived this life, while Barnardo tried hard, and did a better job of helping than others, even his efforts had their limits. We notice that at times the children were placed with families based on the hearsay testimony of another villager. No one from Barnardo's checked out the family or the home in advance. And we see that as time goes on, the visits to the children become further and further apart. And the information gathered regarding the children's well-being becomes less and less detailed. Until finally, the Jackson children pretty much drop off of the Barnardo's radar. Just as untold scores of these children vanished into the Canadian wilderness. Without a trace.

The Jackson's may not have experienced the worst of the possibilities a Home Child could encounter, or maybe they just didn't speak of it. They did nonetheless experience the fear and uncertainty of being taken from their mother and siblings and shipped off to a foreign country to await an unknown fate. They survived, and made it out of the system and on with their lives. But at what cost we will never know.

Most of the children felt loneliness, despair and a need for attention and affection. And since they were English children, from a reserved culture, they were not anxious to talk about their experience. They felt scorn as orphans and waifs, and were treated like a lower class of citizen because of their accent and heritage. For decades they were so ashamed that they didn't speak, even to tell their families. In 1924 the emigration of children under 14 years of age ended, but older than that they kept coming until 1930. Many did indeed help to build the Canadian nation, and many fought in World War One. Heroes of Canada.

SURVEY OF BARNARDO IN CANADA

1868   Jamie Jarvis, first child, emigrated to Canada with Annie MacPherson's Party, Barnardo's first female emigrant followed.

1870   Sprinkling of Barnardo Boys continued to emigrate with Miss Annie MacPherson's emigration parties. Barnardo assists in training programme.

1882   Fifty Barnardo Boys from Stepney Causeway, make up the "Pilgrim Fathers" of Barnardo emigration work into Canada. One hundred Barnardo Boys follow.

1883   First party of 72 Barnardo Girls enter Canada under the care of Miss Emilie Morecroft.

Canadian Agent appointed, A.B. Owen; Canadian Advisory Board formed.

Honourable Senator George A. Cox offers "Hazelbrae", Peterborough to Dr. Barnardo as Canada's first Receiving and Distributing Home.

1912 Renamed the Margaret Cox School for Girls
1929 All Barnardo operations moved to Toronto.

1887   Barnardo travels to Russell, Manitoba, opening site for Industrial Farm For Barnardo Boys. Closed 1904.
Manager Mr. E. A. Struthers Mulock

1889   Barnardo Office and Receiving and Distributing Home for Barnardo Boys opened at Farley Ave., Toronto.

1893   Sir Charles Tupper, Canadian High Commissioner, London encourages Barnardo.

1895	*Ups and Downs,* Canadian Barnardo Publication
1896	Winnipeg Distributing and Receiving Home for Boys and Girls going West. Closed 1918. Manager Mr. E.A.Struthers
1916	Barnardo Emigration to Canada ceases.
1920	First post-war emigration.
1922	New Canadian Headquarters, 538 Jarvis Street, former home of C. Mulock
1926	Prohibition of emigration of children under 14 to Canada
1930	Economic Depression, last supervised Barnardo party.
1939	Final emigration of Barnardo children, 21 boys, 7 girls
1960	Barnardo Office at 466 Briar Hill Avenue, Toronto, closed. All Barnardo records shipped back to England.

BARNARDO EMIGRATION TO CANADA
1867 – 1912

From	1867-1890	1891	1892	1893	1894	1895	1896	1897	1898	1899	1900	1901
Boys	3038	417	596	758	635	578	490	438	371	446	592	698
Girls	1107	5	131	76	89	155	188	226	242	201	339	315
Total	4145	422	727	834	724	733	678	652	613	647	931	1013

	1902	1903	1904	1905	1906	1907	1908	1909	1910	1911	1912	Total
Boys	684	836	863	981	728	742	630	632	630	591	539	16913
Girls	369	401	403	333	443	340	313	335	332	411	374	7128
Total	1053	1237	1266	1314	1171	1082	943	967	962	1002	913	24041

DOCTOR BARNARDO'S "AFTER SAILING" NOTIFICATION

18 to 26 Stepney Causeway,
London, E.
1888

To _____(Parent or Guardian)_____

I am desired to inform you that in accordance with the terms of the agreement entered into when

_____(Name of Child)_____

was received into this Institution, the Managers included her in the party of girls who left these Homes for Canada.

Should you desire to write to her, the address is the

The Secretary, "Dr. Barnardo's Homes, "Hazel-brae, Peterborough, Ontario, Canada. Your letter will need a penny stamp.

Analysis of 1888 Barnardo Emigration Party to Canada

- 22 were between 6 and 12 years old
- 67 were over 12.
- 40 had been in the homes 1 to 3 years
- 20 under 1 year
- 29 over 3 years
- 9   had both parents living
- 16 had fathers only
- 36 had mothers only
- 28 were orphans and some being waif and friendless on admission.
- 42 came from London
- 42 from English counties
- 3   from Ireland
- 1   from Scotland
- 1   from Jersey

Dr. Barnardo's Canadian Headquarters, 1922; 532 Jarvis Street, Toronto, Ontario — Barnardo Archives

Printed in Great Britain
by Amazon.co.uk, Ltd.,
Marston Gate.